W9-CJG-919

Now You're COOKING

HEALTHY RECIPES FROM LATIN AMERICA

BRAZIL

Heidi Krumenauer

PURPLE TOAD
PUBLISHING

P.O. Box 631
Kennett Square, Pennsylvania 19348
www.purpletoadpublishing.com

Now You're COOKING
HEALTHY RECIPES FROM
LATIN AMERICA

Brazil

Cuba

Guatemala

Mexico

Puerto Rico

Printing   1   2   3   4   5   6   7   8   9

Publisher's Cataloging-in-Publication Data
Krumenauer, Heidi
  Brazil / Heidi Krumenauer
    p. cm.—(Now you're cooking. Healthy recipes from Latin America)
Includes bibliographic references and index.
ISBN: 978-1-62469-042-6 (library bound)
1. Cooking, Brazilian—Juvenile literature. 2. Cooking—Juvenile literature. 3. Recipes for health.   I. Title.
 TX716.B6 2013
 641.5981—dc23
                                        2013936076

eBook ISBN: 9781624690433

Printed by Lake Book Manufacturing, Chicago, IL

CONTENTS

Introduction
Brazil:
A Melting Pot of Ethnic Influences

Welcome to Brazil, the largest country in South America and the fifth-largest country in the world! The country lies on the East Coast of South America. About one-fourth of all the world's known plants are found in Brazil. During the 1900s, logging destroyed many of the lush rainforests, leaving dozens of animal and plant species extinct. Although the country's soil is not fertile enough for agriculture in most areas, it is well-suited for growing crops like cocoa, sugar, and coffee. Brazil is also a primary exporter of nuts, soybeans, orange juice, tobacco, and tropical fruits.

The country is divided into five regions: north, northeast, central west, southeast, and south. Each region has a different culture that has been influenced by immigrants from Portugal, Africa, Italy, Germany, Syria, Lebanon, Asia, and Arabia. This diverse mix of international heritage is still present in Brazil's cooking; however, the cuisine varies from region to region.

The North
This area covers the rainforests and tributaries of the Amazon River. The Amazon basin is populated by native Indians or people of mixed Indian and Portuguese descent. They primarily live on a diet of fish, root vegetables, such as manioc, yams, and peanuts, and tropical fruits. One

The Amazon Rainforest is one of Brazil's many singular natural features. The country's population is also comprised of many unique people, such as those who practice Shamanism and are believed to have a connection with the spirit world.

popular dish, *caruru do pará,* is a one-pot meal of dried shrimp, okra, onion, tomato, and coriander.

The Northeast
The semi-arid northeast region is suitable for raising cattle. Dishes typically include dried meat, rice, beans, goat, manioc, and cornmeal. On the coast, sugar cane and cocoa grow abundantly. Seafood, shellfish, and tropical fruits are common staples.

The Central West
This region is made up of dry prairies with woodlands in the north. Regional dishes include fish from the main rivers and beef and pork from ranches. People from this region also eat soybeans, rice, corn, and manioc.

The Southeast
This region has larger cities with several, distinct styles of cooking. In Minas Gerais, the second most populous state in Brazil, the recipes often include corn, pork, beans, and soft cheeses. In the cities of Rio de Janeiro and São Paulo, *feijoada* (bean stew) and *feijao com arroz* (rice and beans) are common dishes. Black or red beans are found in dishes in Minas Gerais. Black beans are common in Rio. Red or white beans are traditional in São Paulo.

The South
The southern region is best suited for raising cattle or growing crops. Dishes are made with sun dried or salt dried beans and *churrasco,* a meal of grilled fresh meats. Immigrants introduced wine, leafy vegetables, and dairy products to the southern Brazilian diet.

Christ the Redeemer is the largest art deco statue in the world. It stands atop the Corcovado mountain in Rio de Janeiro, Brazil. The statue is 98 feet tall and 92 feet wide.

Staples of Brazilian Cuisine: Breakfast

Each region has its own specialty food, but there are a number of staple ingredients that are important to dishes across Brazil. You'll need to stock up on these if you're going to spend time in a Brazilian kitchen!

feijao (beans)—Beans are part of local menus nearly every day. They come in a variety of forms and colors. The *feijao preto* (black bean) is considered the national bean, but it's also easy to find dried red beans, white, brown, pink, black-eyed beans, and chickpeas in local markets.

coconut—Coconut is used in soups, cocktails, poultry, fish, shellfish, and sweet dish recipes. It is used in many forms: *coco verde* (unripe green coconuts); *coco amarelo* (ripe yellow or brown coconuts); *coco de agua* (soft-textured meat of green coconuts); or *coco ralado* (grated coconut).

azeite de dendê (dendê oil)—This tropical oil extracted from the African palm of northern Brazil is a basic ingredient in Bahian or Afro-Brazilian cuisine. It adds rich flavor and a bright orange color to foods.

bacalhau (dried, salted cod)—*Bacalhau* is consumed as an appetizer, soup ingredient, main course, and even as a savory pudding. The fish, with its skin and bone removed, is soaked in cold water for three to four hours before it's ready to eat.

camarão seco (dried shrimp)—Dried shrimp is used largely in Brazil's northern regions. Before cooking, the shrimp are soaked in cold water overnight.

Fresh fruit is always available at local Brazilian markets.

lemon—Most Brazilian recipes contain lemon. In Brazil, lemons are quite green, small, and tart, and are similar to limes as we know them.

arroz brasileiro (Brazilian-style rice)—This long-grained, fluffy rice is briefly sautéed in garlic and oil and then covered with boiling water. Sometimes onion, diced tomatoes, or black olives are added for extra flavor.

farofa or farinha (manioc)—Manioc flour is sautéed in butter until it resembles buttered bread crumbs. *Farinha* is manioc flour sprinkled over rice and beans. *Farofa* is manioc flour sautéed with oil, onions, eggs, olives, and other ingredients.

coffee—Brazil is the world's largest producer of coffee. It is common to see locals, including children, drinking it throughout the day. Brazilians use coffee in their cooking in many distinctive ways.

Pao de Queijo
(Brazilian Cheesy Bread)

Pequeno almoço (breakfast) is a simple meal in Brazil, usually consisting of coffee, milk, bread, and fruit. Brazilians also enjoy a more modest meal of toasted French bread and *café come leite* (coffee with milk) served in bakeries and cafés and more elaborate meals on weekends.

Ingredients

2 cups tapioca flour
2 eggs, beaten
⅔ cup grated Parmesan cheese
⅓ cup milk
½ cup olive oil
2 teaspoons minced garlic
⅓ cup water
1 teaspoon salt

Directions

1. Preheat oven to 375°F.
2. With the help of **an adult,** mix olive oil, milk, salt, and water in a large saucepan. Bring to boil on high heat.
3. Remove from heat immediately. Add flour and garlic. Mix well.
4. Let sit for 10–15 minutes.
5. Add egg and cheese. Stir to form a thick mixture.
6. Drop balls of mixture on a non-greased baking sheet.
7. Bake for 15–20 minutes, or until golden brown.

Makes 10 rolls.

Cheese is a common ingredient found in Brazilian breads.

Empanadas
(Stuffed Bread)

Ingredients

5 large refrigerated biscuits
6 eggs
1 cup chopped chicken
8 oz cheese of your choice
Salt and pepper to taste

Directions

1. With the help of **an adult,** scramble the eggs.
2. Flatten refrigerated biscuits into large circles.
3. Place cheese in center of each circle.
4. Crumble chicken on cheese.
5. Place some scrambled egg on top of chicken.
6. Fold over biscuit and press with a fork to seal sides.
7. Add other chopped ingredients, such as onion, pepper, or cooked shrimp as desired.
8. Bake biscuits as directed on package.

Serves 5.

Empanadas are made by folding dough or bread around stuffing, which usually consists of meats, cheeses, vegetables, or fruits. They are either baked or fried.

Brazilians love *canja de galinha.* It is a chicken rice soup found on restaurant menus across the country. Canja is served as a light entrée and is often eaten before a main course or later in the evening at home. Do you have a sniffle or a sneeze? Here's a cure! Brazilians eat canja to help fight colds, digestive problems, and other mild sicknesses.

Ingredients

3 pounds boneless, skinless chicken meat
1 onion, chopped
6 cups chicken stock
¼ cup brown rice
¾ cup tomato, peeled, seeded, and
    chopped
½ cup chopped carrots
Salt to taste
Ground black pepper to taste
1 tablespoon fresh parsley, chopped

Directions

1. Place chicken, onion, and chicken stock in large saucepan. With the help of **an adult,** bring to a simmer, then cover. Cook over low heat until chicken is tender (about 45 minutes). Lift chicken onto a platter and set aside. Strain stock through a sieve set over a bowl. Discard solids and skim off as much fat as possible from stock.
2. Rinse saucepan and return stock to it. Add rice, tomatoes, and carrots to stock. Season with salt and black pepper to taste. Bring to a simmer. Cook until rice is tender (about 25 minutes).
3. Cut chicken into strips about ½ x 1½ inches after it cools enough to handle. Return chicken to soup and cook just long enough to heat through. Add parsley and serve.

Serves 12.

With a large number of people working outside of the home, soup is a quick, easy meal that is considered a healthy option.

Orange Salad

Many kinds of fruit grow in Brazil, including apples, oranges, peaches, strawberries, bananas, papayas, mangoes, and avocados. Because fruit is so easy to find at feiras (street markets), Brazilians enjoy simple salads made from local produce. Orange salad is often served with feijoada, Brazil's main dish.

Ingredients

5   oranges
1   teaspoon honey
    Salt and pepper to taste

Directions

1. Peel oranges and remove inner cores.
2. Cut oranges into thin slices. Arrange slices on a plate.
3. Drizzle them with honey.
4. Sprinkle salt and pepper over slices to taste.
5. Serve or cover with plastic wrap and refrigerate until ready to eat.

Serves 5.

Brazil is one of the
leading producers
of oranges.

Brazilian Fruit Salad

Ingredients

1   medium ripe pineapple, peeled, cored, and cut into ½-inch pieces
1   medium ripe mango, peeled, pitted, and cut into ½-inch pieces
1   medium ripe papaya, peeled, seeded, and cut into ½-inch pieces
1   seedless orange, peeled and cut into ½-inch pieces
1   banana, peeled and cut into ½-inch pieces
1   medium apple, peeled and cut into ½-inch chunks
    Sweetened condensed milk to taste

Directions

1. In a medium bowl, combine and toss fruit.
2. Drizzle with sweetened condensed milk.

Serves 6.

With so many different types of fruits growing in Brazil, it's easy to have healthy choices available for meals or snacks.

Brazilian Cobb Salad

Ingredients for dressing

⅓ cup chopped cashews
½ cup parsley leaves
4 tablespoons orange juice
3 tablespoons lime juice
½ teaspoon liquid aminos (a liquid soybean protein)
½ teaspoon ground black pepper

Ingredients for salad

½ red onion, thinly sliced in half-rings
8 cups loosely packed mixed greens
1 (14.5 oz) can hearts of palm, rinsed and sliced into rounds
1 green bell pepper, diced
1 red bell pepper, diced
1 avocado, diced
1 cup no-salt-added black beans, drained and cooked
1 cup corn kernels, fresh or frozen and thawed
2 tablespoons cashews

Directions

1. To make dressing, combine all ingredients in a blender and have an adult blend until smooth. Taste and adjust seasoning, and thin to desired consistency by adding orange or lime juice. Transfer to a bowl and set aside.
2. To make salad, place onion slices in water, add a few ice cubes and let sit for at least 15 minutes before serving. When ready to assemble salad, pour off water and drain onion thoroughly. Soaking onion in water reduces its sharpness.
3. To serve, arrange greens on a platter or in a large salad bowl. Arrange onion, hearts of palm, bell peppers, avocado, black beans, corn, and cashews in sections on top of greens. Stir dressing to recombine and serve alongside salad.

Serves 10.

Fresh vegetables are abundant in the various regions of Brazil. They are commonly used in salads.

Main and Side
Dishes for
Lunch and Dinner

The most important meal of the day is eaten at midday or shortly thereafter. For some, it would consist of pasta, meat or fish, along with salad, rice, beans, manioc, and a sweet dessert. For others, the meal would consist mainly of rice and beans. In either case, it is usually followed by a small cup of cafezinho (strong Brazilian coffee). The evening meal is usually much smaller and may include soup or leftovers from earlier in the day.

Between lunch and supper it is customary to have *café,* which includes coffee, hot milk, and cookies. Pastels, small pastries filled with shrimp, meat, and cheese that are either fried or baked, are a favorite snack. These can be purchased from street vendors or made at home.

In the late evening, many Brazilians eat a light supper. Children enjoy desserts such as *pudim* or *churros,* fried dough rolled in sugar and filled with caramel, chocolate, or sweetened condensed milk.

Pepper-Scented Rice

Roman Catholics in Brazil participate in the world-renowned Carnival celebration held each year. Carnival is a week-long party that concludes on Ash Wednesday, the start of the 46-day religious period of Lent, which leads to Easter. During Carnival, children and adults dress in costumes and dance in the streets during the day and night. They eat and drink nearly nonstop, enjoying spicy dishes like pepper-scented rice and feijoada and a variety of sweet dishes, too.

Ingredients

1   tablespoon vegetable oil
1   small onion, finely diced
1   garlic clove, minced
1   cup long-grain rice (brown rice is a healthier alternative)
1   chili pepper
2   cups hot water
½   teaspoon salt

Directions

1. With the help of **an adult,** pour vegetable oil into a large saucepan and heat for a few seconds. Add onion, garlic, and rice.
2. Fry gently, stirring for about 4 minutes.
3. Add chili pepper, hot water, and salt. Stir well and bring to a boil.
4. Simmer for 15–20 minutes until rice is soft and water has been absorbed.
5. Remove chili pepper and serve.

Serves 4.

Carnivals are celebrated in many countries,
but the one in Brazil is the most famous.

25

Polenta
(Fried Cornmeal)

Ingredients

3¼ cups water
¾ teaspoon salt
1 cup whole grain cornmeal

Directions

1. With the help of **an adult,** stir ingredients in a saucepan over medium-high heat until they come to a slow boil.
2. Reduce heat to low, cover and cook for 15 minutes. Stir frequently.
3. Spread polenta in a bread pan.
4. Wait until it is completely cool, then cut into 2-inch-wide slices.
5. Fry in a skillet over medium heat in 2 tablespoons of butter for 10 minutes on each side until crunchy.

Serves 4.

Polenta is a cornmeal that is boiled into a porridge. It can be eaten as a porridge or it can be baked, fried, or grilled.

Feijoada
(Bean Stew)

Feijoada (pronounced fay-JWAH-duh) is Brazil's national dish. It is a recipe of bean stew with rice and pork. Feijoada is thought to have originated during the time of the slave trade where it contained inexpensive and less desirable cuts of meat, such as pig's feet, tail, and nose. Brazilian slaves would create their dish from the leftovers of their masters' tables. The slaves, who worked in cotton fields, cocoa production, and diamond and gold mining, needed energy for the long days.

Today, feijoada consists of a variety of meats slowly cooked with black beans and condiments. Parts like the pig's feet, tail, and nose are no longer added to the dish. It is found in Brazilian restaurants, typically on Wednesdays and Saturdays. Feijoada is made quite often at home, too. Families in Rio de Janeiro are known to eat it at least once a month. They also enjoy feijoada on special occasions, such as Christmas, Easter, and birthdays. Feijoada can be made without meat for a healthier meal, such as the recipe here!

Ingredients

5½ cups dried black beans, rinsed and drained
1 tablespoon canola oil
1 large yellow onion, diced
2 medium red (or green) bell peppers, diced
1 large tomato, diced
4 garlic cloves, minced
1 canned chipotle pepper, chopped
2 cups sweet potatoes (or butternut squash), peeled and diced
2 teaspoons dried (or fresh) thyme leaves
2 teaspoons dried parsley
1 teaspoon salt
4 cups cooked brown rice

Every Brazilian cook has his or her special way of preparing feijoada. No matter who is serving the meal, it's likely that orange slices will accompany this national dish.

Directions

1. In a medium saucepan, place beans in plenty of water and with the help of **an adult,** cook for about 1 hour over medium heat until tender.
2. Drain and reserve 2 cups of cooking liquid.
3. In a large saucepan, heat oil.
4. Add onion, bell peppers, tomato, garlic, and chipotle peppers and sauté for 8–10 minutes.
5. Add beans, cooking liquid, sweet potatoes, and thyme and cook for 25–30 minutes over medium heat, stirring occasionally.
6. Stir in parsley and salt and cook for 5–10 minutes more.
7. Spoon rice into bowls and ladle feijoada over top.

Serves 2.

Camarão na Moranga
(Pumpkin with Shrimp)

Shrimp served in a pumpkin is a traditional food eaten during Brazilian holidays, such as Christmas and New Year's Day, birthdays, anniversaries, and dinner parties. It's a great way to serve larger crowds! Some restaurants serve the dish in miniature pumpkins—the perfect size for one person.

Ingredients

1 medium pumpkin
2 pounds large shrimp, cleaned and deveined, shells saved
3 cups half and half
1 medium onion, divided
3 large garlic cloves, peeled
2 bay leaves
½ teaspoon freshly ground nutmeg
Salt and pepper
2 tablespoons all-purpose flour
2 tablespoons olive oil
3 sprigs rosemary, chopped
10 large Roma tomatoes, chopped
1 cup cilantro, roughly chopped
8 oz cream cheese (can be low fat
    cream cheese)

Directions

1. Preheat oven to 350°F.
2. With the help of **an adult,** cut top of pumpkin and remove all seeds. Wrap pumpkin in aluminum foil and place on a large shallow ovenproof pan, cut-off side down. Bake until soft (about 45–60 minutes). Remove from oven and carefully remove foil. Set aside.
3. In a medium sauce pan, add shrimp shells, half and half, half of onion, 2 garlic cloves, and bay leaves. Season with nutmeg, salt, and pepper. Cook on medium heat until liquid is reduced to half

(about 25 minutes). Remove from heat and stain out all the solids and discard them. Whisk the flour into the liquid and set aside.

4. Finely chop remaining onion and garlic. With the help of an adult, heat olive oil on medium high heat in a large pan. Cook onion until soft (about 3 minutes). Add garlic and rosemary and cook until fragrant (about 40 seconds). Stir in tomatoes, close lid, and cook for 5 minutes. Remove lid and smash tomatoes with a potato masher. Close lid, reduce heat to medium low, and cook for another 25 minutes. Constantly stirring, add white sauce and cook until it thickens. Add shrimp and cook for another 5 minutes, or until the shrimp turn pink and start to curl. Remove from heat and fold in cilantro. Set aside.

5. With a spoon, spread cream cheese into the pumpkin's inside wall. Add shrimp sauce inside pumpkin and place back into the oven. Bake for another 15–20 minutes, or until cheese starts to melt.

6. Carefully place whole pumpkin on a serving dish on table. To serve, scoop shrimp mixture out making sure to bring some chunks of melted pumpkin and cream cheese with it. Serve over a bed of brown rice.

Serves 12.

Desserts
Banana Frita
(Fried Banana)

Ingredients

2 ripe bananas
2 teaspoons butter
Cinnamon and sugar to taste

Directions

1. Peel bananas.
2. With the help of an adult, heat butter in a nonstick frying pan.
3. Add bananas and fry on both sides.
4. Remove and sprinkle cinnamon and sugar on top.

Serves 2.

Variation: Add honey and raisins to bananas when frying.

Though Brazilians enjoy using sugar in many of their dishes—especially desserts—there are many traditional, healthier options, such as fried bananas.

Brigadeiro
(Chocolate Bonbon)

Brigadeiro is a popular candy in Brazil and Portugal and is usually served at birthday parties. This chocolate bonbon, created in the 1940s, was named after Brigadier Eduardo Gomes, a Brazilian politician and military figure.

Ingredients

1   can (14 oz) condensed milk
4   tablespoons cocoa powder
1   tablespoon butter
    Chocolate sprinkles

Directions

1. Put all ingredients, except chocolate sprinkles, in a microwavable bowl.
2. Microwave on high for 3 minutes.
3. Heat for another 3 minutes on high.
4. Mix well and let cool.
5. Make balls about 1 inch in diameter.
6. Roll in sprinkles. Keep cool.

Serves 4.

Brazil only produces five percent of the world's cocoa. It's large production dropped after disease spread through the Bahia region in 1989.

Bolo Pamonha
(Corn Cake)

Festas Juninas (June festivals) are held in honor of Roman Catholic saints—St. Anthony, St. Peter, and St. John. Brazilians believe St. John protects corn and green bean harvests, giving them plenty of food in the upcoming year. They celebrate St. John's Day with a harvest festival. Brazilians like to eat corn, as corn-on-the-cob and popcorn, and corn-based dishes, such as corn puddings and corn cake, during the festivals.

Ingredients

1 can (11 0z) corn, drained
7 tablespoons softened butter
1 cup whole wheat flour
3 eggs, beaten
1 can (14 oz) coconut milk
1 tablespoon baking powder
2 cups granulated sugar

Directions

1. Preheat oven to 350°F.
2. Place all dry ingredients into a bowl and mix. Slowly add milk, eggs, butter, and corn. Mix until smooth.
3. Pour mixture into a large greased loaf pan.
4. Bake for about 50 minutes.
5. To test if cake is done, stick a toothpick into its center. The cake is done when the toothpick comes out clean.
6. Remove cake from pan by turning it over onto a wire rack to cool.
7. Slice and serve.

Serves 8.

Brazil corn production continues to rise. In 2013, the country experienced a record crop.

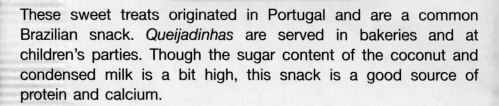

Queijadinhas (Coconut and Cheese Treats)

These sweet treats originated in Portugal and are a common Brazilian snack. *Queijadinhas* are served in bakeries and at children's parties. Though the sugar content of the coconut and condensed milk is a bit high, this snack is a good source of protein and calcium.

Ingredients

1 cup tightly-packed, fresh-grated coconut
1 can (8 oz) sweetened condensed milk
2 tablespoons freshly-grated Parmesan cheese
2 large egg yolks

Directions

1. Preheat oven to 450°F.
2. Place all ingredients in a medium-sized bowl and mix well.
3. Place paper cups into cups of a muffin tin. Drop mixture by the spoonful into paper cups.
4. Place muffin tin in a larger pan that has been filled with about 1 inch of water and cook for about 35 minutes.
5. For best freshness, store in air-tight container.

Serves 12.

There are many types of queijadinhas, but the traditional recipe is prepared with coconut, cheese, sweetened condensed milk, sugar, butter, and egg yolks.

Pineapple-Orange Drink

The Portuguese brought oranges and other citrus fruits to Brazil in 1500. They are now used in many dishes and juices. This pineapple-orange drink can be enjoyed as an after-school snack or anytime!

Ingredients

2   tablespoons crushed ice
2   tablespoons sparkling (or seltzer) water
½   cup orange juice
½   cup pineapple juice

Directions

1. Pour crushed ice and water into a large drinking glass.
2. Add orange juice and pineapple juice.
3. Stir and drink.

Variation: Have **an adult** make the juice in a blender.

Brazilians eat large amounts of pineapple. It is affordable and available year-round.

Customs, Celebrations, and Traditions

Christmas

On Christmas Day, it is tradition for the main meal to be served late at night on Christmas Eve. The meal is known as *ceia de Natal* (Christmas dinner). Brazilians often serve bacalhau and peru (turkey). The turkey is often basted with a rich, dark coffee combined with cream and sugar. The traditional stuffing contains farofa, pork sausage, onions, celery, and seasonings. Side dishes include mashed white sweet potatoes, bananas fritas, and green beans. Dessert is typically an assortment of *fruit doces* (sweetened fruits, preserved through slow cooking), star fruit, and strips of mango.

Eating Out

In the cities, it is common to eat midday *lanches* (meaning "lunches"), which are smaller meals in restaurants that serve food similar to the United States. *Pizzarias* offer pizza and pasta. Churrascarias offer barbeque, sides, and salad bars. A *lanchonete* is a snack bar that offers sandwiches, hamburgers, pastries, and other readymade snacks. Respect the Brazilian custom of not eating "on the go". If you stop for a snack or coffee, it is courteous to finish it before you start wandering down the street.

Some Brazilians eat their noon meal at home or bring their lunch to work. Soft drinks and bottled water often accompany the meal.

Etiquette

Since dinner is served later in the evening, it's common to spot children in restaurants at all hours. Because Brazilian children

frequently dine with their parents. They learn table manners and etiquette at an early age. Using utensils properly is just one of their many lessons. Brazilians don't use their hands as much as Americans do when eating their food. In fact, they usually use a fork and knife for pizza, open sandwiches, and chicken. The fork is held in the left hand and the knife in the right. If you're a leftie, feel free to break that rule!

Books

Fernando, Farah. *The Food and Cooking of Brazil: Traditions, Ingredients, Tastes, Techniques, 65 Classic Recipes.* Wigston, Leicester: Anness, 2012.

Peterson, Joan and David Peterson. *Eat Smart in Brazil: How to Decipher the Menu, Know the Market Foods & Embark on a Tasting Adventure* (Eat Smart Series, No. 1). Madison, WI: Ginkgo Press, 1995.

Sheen, Barbara. *Foods of Brazil (Taste of Culture).* San Diego: Kidhaven Press, 2007.

Works Consulted

Brazilian Eating Habits
http://www.maria-brazil.org/brazilian_eating_habits.htm

Celebrate Brazil
http://www.celebratebrazil.com/brazil-food.html

Countries and Their Cultures: Brazil
http://www.everyculture.com/Bo-Co/Brazil.html#b

Flavors of Brazil
http://flavorsofbrazil.blogspot.com

Food in Every Country
http://www.foodbycountry.com/Algeria-to-France/Brazil.html

World Cup 2014 Traveler's Guide
http://www.worldcupriobrazil.com/cat egory/food_bevarage/

On the Internet

Brazilian Breakfast

    http://www.buzzle.com/articles/brazilian-breakfast.html

Brazilian Brigadeiro

    http://www.food.com/recipe/
    brazilian-brigadeiro-microwave-289515?oc=linkback

Brazilian Cobb Salad

    http://www.wholefoodsmarket.com/recipe/brazilian-cobb-salad

Brazilian Feijoada (Vegetarian)

    http://www.food.com/recipe/brazilian-feijoada-vegetarian-455068

Brazilian Fruit Salad

    http://cuposugar.blogspot.com/2008/03/brazilian-fruit-salad.html

Brazilian Pineapple-Orange

    http://www.food.com/recipe/pineapple-orange-drink-brazilian-
    456874

Brazil Recipes

    http://www.foodbycountry.com/Algeria-to-France/Brazil.html#b

Canja

    http://allrecipes.com/recipe/canja/detail.aspx

Pumpkin with Shrimp

    http://www.cynthiapresser.com/recipe-blog/main-dishes/
    fish-a-seafood/160-pumpkin-with-shrimp-camarao-na-moranga

cuisine (kwih-ZEEN)—A type of food from a certain place.

entrée (AHN-tray)—The main dish of a meal.

etiquette (EH-tih-kit)—Rules on how to behave properly, especially while eating.

sauté (saw-TAY)—To fry in a small amount of fat.

scramble (SKRAM-bull)—To mix up.

simmer—To be cooked gently or remain just at or below the boiling point.

traditional (truh-DISH-uh-nul)—An inherited, established, or customary pattern of thought, action, or behavior, such as a religious practice or a social custom.

A toucan in the rainforest

Heidi Krumenauer has written over 1,200 newspaper and magazine articles. She has contributed chapters to 17 book projects, including several for the *Chicken Soup for the Soul* series. Her first book, *Why Does Grandma Have a Wibble?* was released in 2007. Krumenauer has also written several youth biographies: *Brett Favre, Carly Rae Jepsen, Flo Rida, Harry Styles of One Direction, Jimmie Johnson, Joe Flacco, Lady Gaga, Michael Strahan, Rihanna,* and *Sean Kingston*. She is a 1991 graduate of the University of Wisconsin-Platteville and is in upper management with a Fortune 400 insurance company. She and her husband, Jeff, raise their two sons, Noah and Payton, in southern Wisconsin.